Daw, Nicky
    The Vet.—(BEANS. People at work)
    1. Veterinary medicine—Great Britain—
Juvenile literature
    I. Title
    636.089'0941   SF657

    ISBN 0–7136–2700–X

A & C Black (Publishers) Limited
35 Bedford Row, London WC1R 4JH

© 1985 A & C Black (Publishers) Limited

ISBN 0-7136-2700-X

Filmset by August Filmsetting, Haydock, St. Helens.
Printed in Hong Kong by Dai Nippon Printing Co. Ltd.

The Vet

Nicky Daw

Photographs by Chris Fairclough

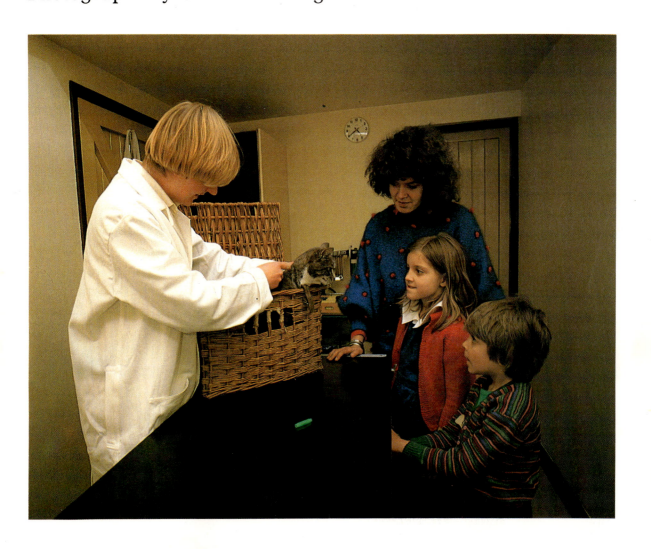

A & C Black · London

Denise has been a vet for five years. It's hard work and she had to study for six years before she could become a vet. But Denise really enjoys her job.

Denise lives just outside a small market town near the Welsh Border. She likes working here because there are farm animals to look after as well as pets.

The surgery where Denise works belongs to another vet called Paul. Paul and Denise share the work between them, and their assistant, Sue, helps them both at the surgery.

Next to the surgery there is a small cottage where Denise lives. She doesn't have far to go to work in the morning, but Denise likes to get up early so that she can take Tally, her golden labrador, for a run. When they get back, they are both ready for a big breakfast.

This morning the phone is ringing just as Denise gets to the surgery. It's a farmer phoning. One of his calves has a lump on its jaw. Can Denise call later in the morning? Denise arranges a time to visit the farm after morning surgery.

During the next half hour, there are quite a few phone calls from people who want to make appointments for their animals to be seen by the vet. Small animals are brought to the surgery but Denise has to arrange to visit large animals. One of the reasons why Denise enjoys being a vet is that each day is different. She never knows what's going to happen next.

The surgery is open every morning and evening. Today, Denise's first visitor is Mr Barker who has brought his seven week-old lamb to be examined. They take the lamb across the yard to the stable where farm animals are looked after, and Mr Barker tells Denise its symptoms. Some of his lambs have scour, the name for diarrohea in animals, but this lamb is the worst.

Denise takes the lamb's temperature. She puts the thermometer up its rectum, not in its mouth, because the lamb would probably bite the thermometer. This is how vets always take an animal's temperature. The lamb looks very miserable and Denise is not suprised to find that its temperature is 105° Fahrenheit. This is three degrees above the normal temperature for a lamb.

After listening to its heartbeat, Denise takes a tiny sample of the lamb's diarrohea and streaks it straight onto a small glass slide.

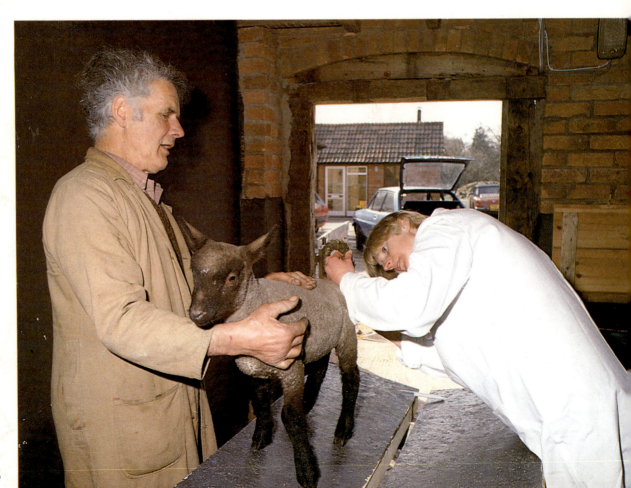

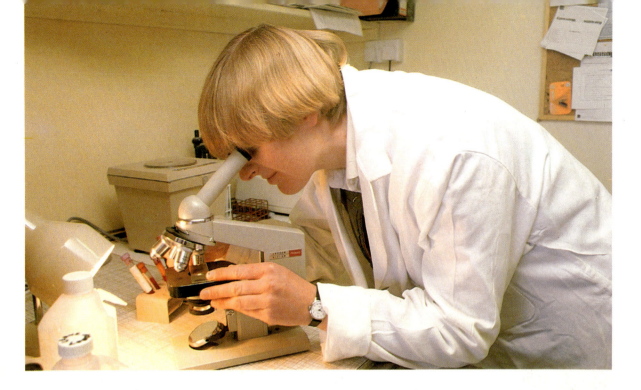

In her laboratory next to the stable, Denise examines the slide underneath the microscope. She is trying to find out whether the lamb has coccidiosis. This is an infection caused by a tiny worm which can live in the intestine and often makes young animals ill. Luckily, there are no coccidia in the sample on the slide and Denise tells Mr Barker that the lamb has some kind of infection. Nevertheless, they must get the lamb better quickly, as young animals with scour can easily die.

Denise gives the lamb an injection of antibiotic to bring down its temperature. Then she gives the lamb a drench. Drench is the name for a medicine which animals can swallow. This will get rid of the infection in the lamb's intestine. As Mr Barker has not let the lamb get too ill before bringing it in, it should be well again in a few days' time.

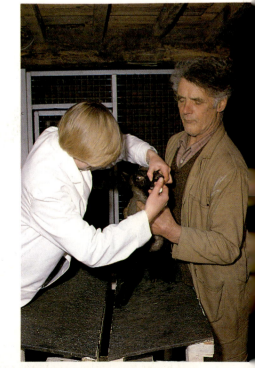

The next job is a sad one. Mrs Bevan has brought in her cat, Marmaduke. He is twelve years old and has been very ill. Denise has done all she can for Marmaduke, but she tells Mrs Bevan that he will not live for very much longer as he is so weak.

Now Marmaduke is in pain and won't eat, so Mrs Bevan doesn't want him to suffer any more. Denise is going to put Marmaduke 'to sleep'. To do this she will give him an injection which will quickly make him fall into a deep sleep and then die peacefully. Mrs Bevan feels very sad as Marmaduke has been part of the family for so long. But Denise is kind and gentle with him and Mrs Bevan stays with him while he has the injection.

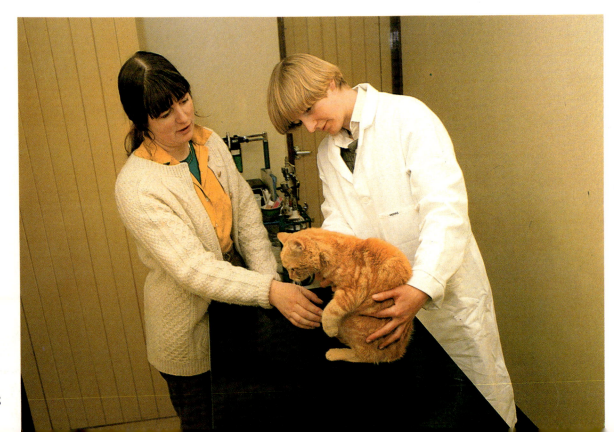

Denise's next patient is another cat which was hit by a car eight weeks ago and had her leg broken. The cat, Twinkle, had to have a metal pin put in her leg to hold the broken bones together. Unfortunately, the pin started to work its way out before the leg had completely healed. So Denise had to take out the pin and put on a plaster.

Now Denise is going to X-ray the leg, just to make sure it has healed properly. First of all, she gives Twinkle a sedative to make her dozy. Then she cuts off the plaster.

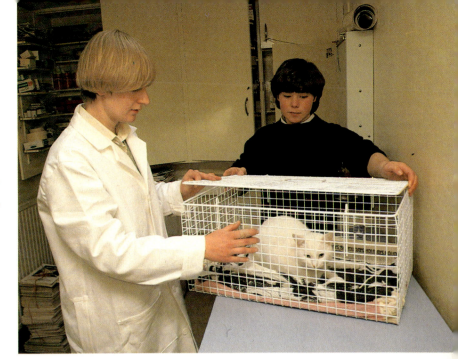

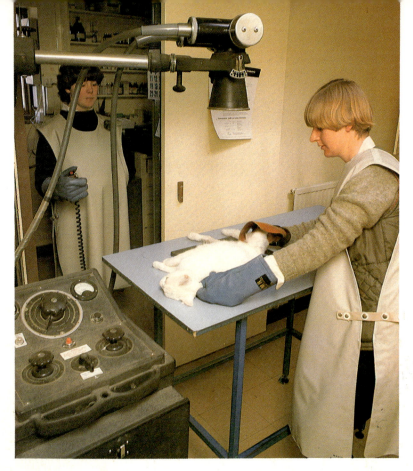

Denise puts on her special radiation-proof coat and lead-lined gloves. She has to do a lot of X-rays and her special clothes stop her from getting too much radiation. Denise lays Twinkle on the X-ray plate while Sue holds the timer and presses it for a split second.

It takes ten minutes for the X-ray to develop. While she's waiting, Denise has a look at the X-ray she took three weeks ago, after she had taken the pin out of Twinkle's leg. She can see exactly where the break was. When the new X-ray is developed, Denise is satisfied that the leg has completely healed. She goes to telephone Twinkle's owner to tell her the good news.

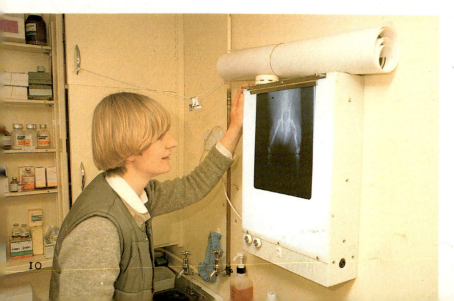

It is now 10.30 in the morning. Denise has a quick coffee, and gets ready for her first home visit. She is going to see the calf with the lump on its jaw. She makes sure that everything, including Tally, is in the car.

Last of all she checks that her 'bleeper' is working. This is a radio which she carries with her whenever she's away from the surgery. If Sue gets an emergency call at the surgery she can 'bleep' Denise. When Denise hears the radio bleep, she knows that she must phone Sue at the surgery as soon as possible.

Half an hour later, Denise and Tally arrive at Mrs Hawk's house. Denise puts on waders and a waterproof jacket to protect her clothes. Mrs Hawk helps to hold the calf which is not at all keen on having its painful jaw prodded by a vet.

As Denise thought, the calf has an abscess. This is like a large boil and it probably started from dirt getting into a scratch. Denise has to clip away the hair from around the abscess and clean the skin. Then she lances the abscess by cutting a slit in it so that she can draw out the pus. Denise injects antiseptic solution into the wound to flush it out. She sprays a special purple antibiotic all over the wound which makes the calf look very odd.

All Denise has to do now is clean herself up – a very important part of a vet's life. She always carries a bucket, brush and disinfectant in her car and she wears the waders and waterproof jacket because they are easy to hose down. This stops her from carrying infection from one farm to another.

Mrs Hawk offers Denise a cup of tea. Usually Denise has to rush off, as she has other farms to visit. But this time she can say yes. Afterwards, Denise gives Mrs Hawk some syringes and a bottle of antibiotic. Mrs Hawk must inject the calf once a day for five days. If the calf doesn't get better quickly, she will have to get in touch with Denise at the surgery.

It is now about midday and Denise wants to fit in one more visit before going back to the surgery. She is going to a farm to do tuberculosis and brucellosis tests on some cows.

Before Denise has a chance to test the cows, the farmer whisks her away to a far corner of the barn. One of the Ryeland ewes is giving birth to a lamb. Denise can see that the ewe is having difficulty lambing and there is no time to lose. She manages to reach up inside the ewe and feel the lamb. One of the lamb's front legs is bent back and the lamb has got stuck. Denise has to push the lamb back a little and then gently unbend the front leg.

The lamb is born, feet first, quite quickly now but both the lamb and its mother are exhausted by the long labour and the lamb hasn't started breathing. Denise puts a piece of straw up its nostril. Sometimes the sudden tickle will make a lamb start to breathe. But this time, it doesn't work. Denise tries another trick. She pours cold water into its ear and the lamb jerks into life. What a relief!

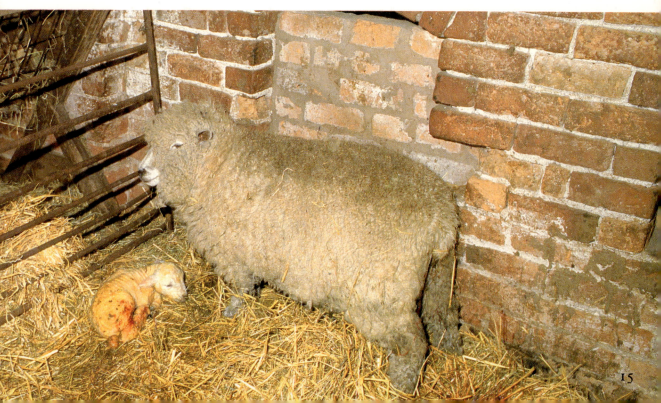

At the other end of the barn is one of Denise's most unusual patients. It's a tiny fallow deer which the farmer's children found a few weeks ago. The deer's leg was caught in a snare and was so badly injured that Denise had to amputate it. Now she checks to see that the stump is healing properly.

Everything is going well but the little deer is still finding it difficult to hop around. It's only just beginning to trust people. The deer will never be able to fend for itself in the wild and will always have to be looked after. But luckily, the Jones family really enjoy caring for the shy little animal.

Now Denise has to test the cows – the real reason
for her visit. Tuberculosis and brucellosis are
serious diseases which can be passed on to people
from cows' milk, so the tests are very important.
Denise has to take blood samples from each cow
and then send them away to be analysed at a
government laboratory.

When she has finished, Denise goes back to the
surgery. She wants to have a quick lunch before the
main event of the day, an operation on a dog. This
will take up most of the afternoon.

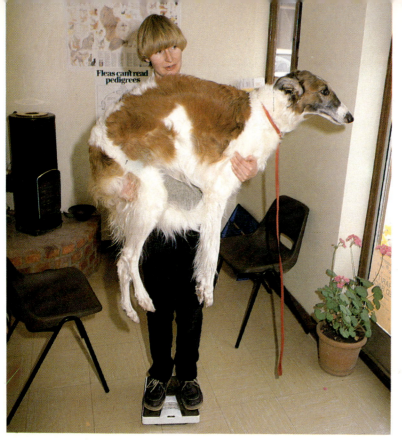

Penny, a borzoi bitch, has an infected uterus (womb). Paul and Denise have to operate on Penny to take the uterus out. Penny will need to have an anaesthetic so that she won't feel anything. The anaesthetic will make her unconscious. Anaesthetics sometimes make animals sick, so Penny hasn't had anything to eat for the last twelve hours. If she was sick while she was unconscious, she might choke.

Now Denise has to weigh Penny so that she can find out how much anaesthetic to give her. Penny's owner stays with Penny while Denise gives her the anaesthetic.

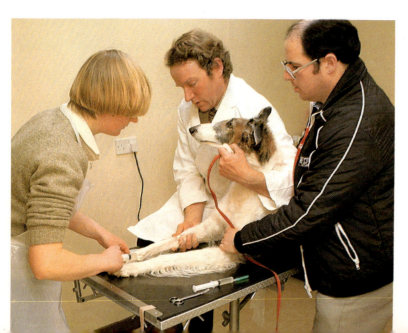

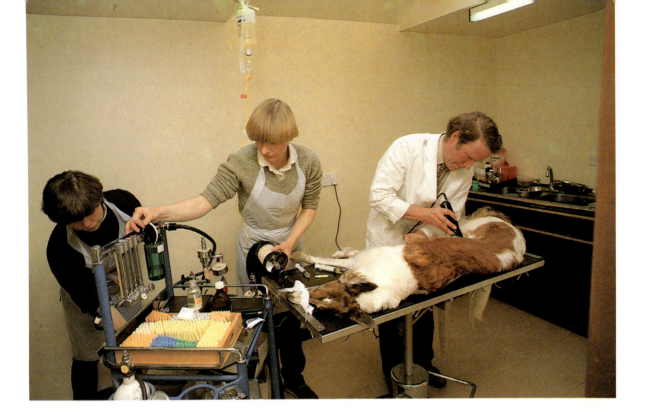

While Paul removes the infected uterus, Denise keeps a careful watch on Penny's breathing. The operation is quite fiddly and takes a long time. But everything goes well. Afterwards the wound is stitched up and cleaned and Penny is given an antibiotic injection. Penny will start to come round in half an hour, but she will stay in the surgery overnight so that Denise and Paul can keep an eye on her.

When the operation is over, Sue sterilises all the instruments which have been used. There musn't be any germs left on the instruments because they could infect the next animal that has an operation. To sterilise the instruments, Sue boils them up in a special pressure cooker and then seals them in germ-free bags.

The operation has taken all afternoon and Denise is tired. She has an hour before evening surgery, so she takes Tally for a walk. Fortunately, evening surgery looks as if it is going to be quiet.

At 4.30 in the afternoon Emily and Henry and their mum arrive with Smoky, the cat. Once a year, Smoky has to have an injection against cat flu and enteritus, a dangerous cat illness. Smoky knows Denise only too well, as he came to the surgery recently with a badly cut paw. Because he remembers this, he starts to miaow even before Denise has touched him with the needle. But he only feels a quick pin-prick before he is put back in his basket.

After washing her hands, Denise fills in Smoky's record card. All Denise's patients have a record card which shows what vaccinations and treatment they've had.

Denise has known Emily and Henry since they were very small and has often given them advice on how to look after their pets. Back in the waiting room, she gives Emily some worming pills for Smoky and explains why it is so important to treat their cat regularly. These pills get rid of the worms which live in dogs' and cats' intestines. If they aren't treated, pets can get very thin and out of condition. The worms can be passed on to human beings too, especially children who spend a lot of time with their pets.

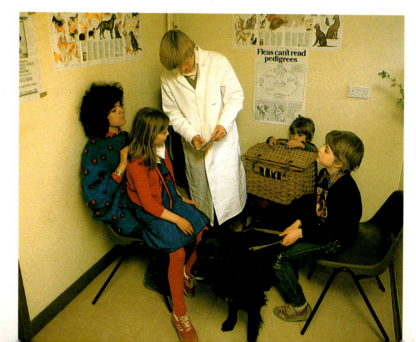

The day's work is over. Denise has the rest of the evening off to go and see her boyfriend, David. He is a shepherd at a nearby hill farm. On the way to David's house Denise's 'bleeper' goes. Quickly, Denise finds a telephone box and phones the surgery. Paul's wife explains that Paul is out seeing a sick cow and now they have had another urgent call. A horse has injured its leg. Can Denise call at the stables as it is not too far from David's house?

It's dark by the time Denise gets to the stables. The horse, Red Knight, caught his leg on a piece of barbed wire while jumping over a fence. The cut is quite deep and very dirty. Denise injects a sedative into a vein in Red Knight's neck and, almost immediately, the horse becomes dozy. Denise warns the groom that Red Knight may want to rest his head on her shoulder.

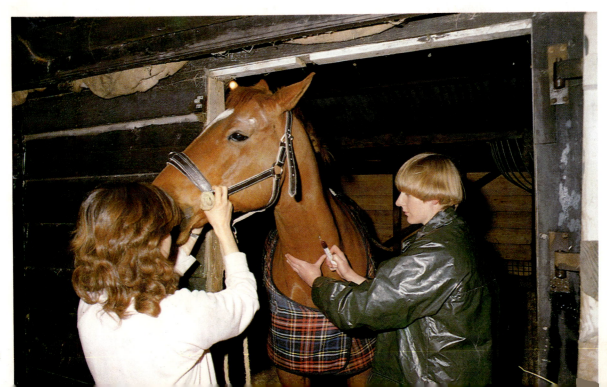

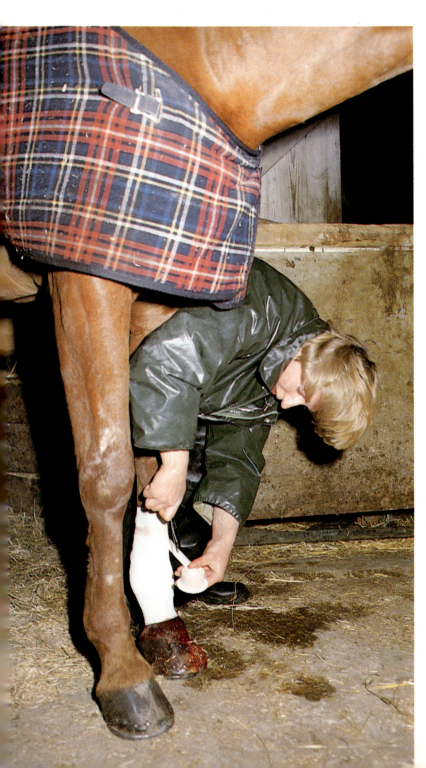

Even though he's sedated, Red Knight is still restless. Denise injects a local anaesthetic all round the cut to make it go numb. She has to be careful that Red Knight doesn't stamp on her foot. After cleaning the wound and stitching it up, Denise gives Red Knight two injections. One injection is a vaccination against tetanus and the other is penicillin to stop any infection. Then she carefully bandages the horse's leg.

It is the end of a long, hard but satisfying day. Denise fills in Red Knight's record card and hoses herself down. Then she sets off again. She stops only to ring David and tell him that she'll be arriving soon, and that she's very hungry indeed. David tells her that he's made supper but would Denise mind just popping out to the barn when she gets there as one of his lambing ewes is poorly? 'It's a good thing I enjoy being a vet,' laughs Denise. 'I'll be round in 24 ten minutes.'